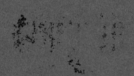

TITLE I
HOLMES JR HIGH
2001-02

CREATIVE EDUCATION

CAROLINA PANTHERS

JOHN NICHOLS

Published by Creative Education
123 South Broad Street, Mankato, Minnesota 56001
Creative Education is an imprint of The Creative Company

Designed by Rita Marshall

Photos by: Allsport USA, SportsChrome

Library of Congress Cataloging-in-Publication Data

Nichols, John, 1966–
Carolina Panthers / by John Nichols.
p. cm. — (NFL today)
Summary: Traces the history of the team from its beginnings through 1999.
ISBN 1-58341-038-4

1. Carolina Panthers (Football team)—History—Juvenile literature. [1. Carolina
Panthers (Football team)—History. 2. Football—History.] I. Title. II. Series:
NFL today (Mankato, Minn.)

GV956.C27N53   2000
796.332'64'09756—dc21   99-015744

First edition

9 8 7 6 5 4 3 2 1

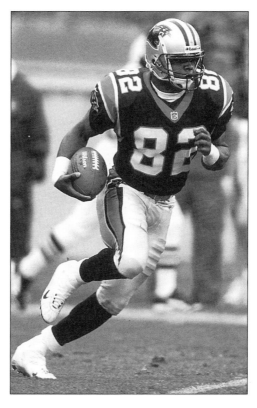

Charlotte, North Carolina, is one of America's fastest-growing cities. Thousands of people come to the Charlotte metropolitan area every day to do business, and many settle there. Visitors are impressed by the city's blend of traditional Southern grace and modern attitude. It is the third-largest banking center in the United States and a leader in manufacturing as well.

While Charlotte has experienced a major growth spurt only in recent years, the city has a long and storied history. It was founded by British settlers in 1746 and named after the wife of King George III of England. Despite their town's

Speedy kick return specialist Michael Bates.

Cornerback Tim McKyer intercepted three passes, returning one 96 yards for a touchdown.

connection to English rulers, the citizens of Charlotte were fiercely anti-British during the American Revolution. British general Cornwallis later called the town a "hornet's nest" because of the stinging blows that local soldiers struck against his army. Charlotte's citizens have always been proud of Cornwallis's remark. When the city was looking for a good name for its new professional basketball team in the late 1980s, the choice was obvious: the Hornets.

Charlotte's basketball team was an immediate success and set records for fan attendance. National Football League officials took note of this. When the league began making plans to award two new expansion franchises, it welcomed a bid from Charlotte-area business leaders. In October 1993, the NFL made the Carolina Panthers its 29th franchise.

That was only the start, however. The club was scheduled to begin play in September 1995. That meant that, in less than two years' time, a coaching staff and management team had to be put together, players had to be drafted and signed, construction had to begin on a new stadium, and fans had to be won over for a new sports adventure in the Southeast. All of that was accomplished . . . and more.

JERRY RICHARDSON SCORES BIG

The Panthers who took the field at the start of the 1995 season were a blend of veterans and rookies hoping to establish something special together. They included veteran quarterback Frank Reich and rookie signal-caller Kerry Collins; longtime pros such as receivers Don Beebe and Mark Carrier, tight end Pete Metzelaars, safety Brett Maxie,

Tight end Wesley Walls was Carolina's top receiving threat.

Quarterback Frank Reich gave the Panthers veteran leadership in their opening season.

linebacker Lamar Lathon, and placekicker John Kasay; as well as youngsters such as offensive lineman Blake Brockermeyer and defensive back Tyrone Poole.

These football heroes were similar to the pioneers who settled the town of Charlotte more than 250 years ago. Panthers fans hope that these football pioneers have laid the groundwork for great things to come in North Carolina. The real pioneer of professional football in the Carolinas was Jerry Richardson, a former pro wide receiver turned millionaire businessman. Richardson's journey from football player to football owner took nearly 35 years.

Richardson was born in a small town in North Carolina and attended Wofford College in Spartanburg, South Carolina, where he earned small college All-American honors. He often dreamed about playing professional football, and he got that chance with the Baltimore Colts for two seasons: 1959 and 1960.

Richardson was a long shot to make the Colts' 1959 roster. "The first day in camp," he recalled, "Baltimore coach Weeb Ewbank said he planned to keep just two wide receivers, and 19 were in camp. Two of them were [future Pro Football Hall of Fame players] Raymond Berry and Lenny Moore, so I wasn't bursting with enthusiasm at my chances."

Nevertheless, Richardson made the team and was named the club's top rookie that year. He even caught a touchdown pass in Baltimore's 31–16 victory over the New York Giants for the 1959 NFL championship. "That pass has become legendary—in the Richardson family," he noted with a smile.

Each Colts player received $4,864 as a winner's bonus, and Richardson decided to invest his money. He joined with a friend to buy the first Hardees restaurant franchise, which opened in Spartanburg in October 1961. Richardson then retired from football to concentrate on business.

But pro football continued to occupy a prominent place in Richardson's heart, and he began to think about owning a team that would represent both North and South Carolina. "This region and its people have been so good to me and my family that there was never any question of what we wanted to do," Richardson said. "My dream was returning something to this special area."

1 9 9 5

Eric Guliford gained 919 combined yards on receptions and punt returns.

The dream started to take shape in 1987, when the NFL announced a competition to determine which two cities would be awarded expansion franchises in the early 1990s. Richardson and his son Mark gathered a group of Charlotte business leaders to head the city's entry into the competition.

After the group was formed, Mark Richardson went to Kansas City to meet with architects who would draw up plans for a state-of-the-art NFL stadium to be built in the Charlotte area. Meanwhile, Jerry Richardson began drawing up plans to finance the expansion franchise and to convince the NFL that Charlotte was the right place to locate a new team. On December 15, 1987, father and son, representing a new group called Richardson Sports, officially announced Charlotte's entry into the NFL sweepstakes.

By 1991, Richardson's quest to bring pro football to North Carolina began to pick up steam. In March, the NFL announced that it had trimmed its list of potential expansion sites down to seven, and Carolina had made the cut. By May, the list was down to five. More than two years passed, but finally, in October 1993, Richardson's dream came true.

10 *Linebacker Sam Mills was the heart of the Panthers defense.*

Powerful nose tackle Greg Kragen.

The NFL announced that the Carolina Panthers would be one of two new franchises to begin play in 1995.

"It's a moment I've been waiting six years for, and you bet it's sweet," exclaimed the happy new owner. "It's a very proud moment for me and my family."

Coach Dom Capers led the Panthers to an NFL-record 12–4 second-season record.

THE ROAD TO VICTORY

Having secured a franchise, Richardson had less than two years to assemble a team. The Panthers were assigned to the Western Division of the league's National Football Conference, placing them in the same division as the mighty San Francisco 49ers. "Being in with the 49ers provides us with an instant challenge," Richardson said. "We're in with the best, and we better get ready."

The plan for the new organization would be to build a top-notch front office and to hire an innovative coach who could construct a competitive team from scratch. First, the Panthers hired Bill Polian as the club's general manager. Polian was an outstanding judge of football talent. He had earlier helped transform the Buffalo Bills from one of the worst teams in the American Football Conference to a four-time AFC champion and the only team ever to play in four consecutive Super Bowls.

Despite his success in Buffalo, Polian lost his job when the Bills were unable to overcome their Super Bowl jinx and win any of their appearances in the title game. Buffalo owner Ralph Wilson felt that changing general managers might alter the team's luck, so he fired Polian. The Panthers jumped at the chance to bring Polian on board in Charlotte.

"The Panthers have hired absolutely the best general manager available," said Buffalo coach Marv Levy, who worked with Polian for many years. "They have taken the right step to come into the NFL today."

Polian's main concerns when he arrived in Charlotte were to hire a coach for the Panthers and to put together the team's first roster. The man he had in mind to lead the club on the field was Dom Capers, who had served as defensive coordinator for the Pittsburgh Steelers since 1992. What most impressed Polian about the 44-year-old Capers was his work ethic. No one put in more hours at his craft than Capers.

"Football is a way of life," Capers once said. "However long it takes to get the job done, we'll do it. The most important thing is for us to be as well-prepared on Sunday as

1 9 9 6

Running back Anthony Johnson exploded for 1,120 rushing yards and six touchdowns.

One of the NFL's most accurate kickers, John Kasay.

we can be. We can't ever relax. If we don't take care of the little things, then we aren't going to be in a position to make a play at the end to win the game."

Capers's players in Pittsburgh respected him as both a coach and a person. "There's no barking at people, no cursing you out," linebacker Levon Kirkland said. "He just coaches you. If he sees something, he'll tell you like a man."

After nearly 25 years as an assistant, Capers was certain that he was ready to be an NFL head coach. Bill Polian and Jerry Richardson agreed, and they offered him the job.

1 9 9 6

Strong safety Brett Maxie led a defense that picked off 22 passes during the regular season.

THE PANTHERS COME TOGETHER

Capers joined the Panthers on January 23, 1995, only days after the Steelers were eliminated from the play-offs in the AFC championship game. Characteristically, he didn't waste any time. The next day, he appointed his coaching staff and met with Bill Polian and his scouts, who had been studying potential players for the Panthers on other NFL teams and on college squads around the country.

Carolina had three ways to select players to fill out its roster. First, there was an expansion draft, with each of the league's 28 existing teams making available some of its unwanted players for the Panthers and fellow expansion team Jacksonville Jaguars to choose from. Second, there was the 1995 spring draft of college players, with the Panthers having the first or second pick in each round. Third, there was the opportunity to sign free agents who had decided not to re-sign with their former teams and might welcome a chance to get more playing time or money in Carolina.

A great Panthers receiver, Mark Carrier.

One of the original Panthers, quarterback Frank Reich.

The expansion draft was held in February 1995, and the Panthers found several quality players among the castoffs from other teams. These included cornerbacks Rod Smith and Tim McKyer, receiver Mark Carrier, and defensive tackle Greg Kragen. McKyer, who had played in two Super Bowls with the San Francisco 49ers and then anchored Pittsburgh's defensive backfield under Capers, was chosen to provide both performance and leadership in the Carolina secondary. Carrier, a former All-Pro receiver with Tampa Bay, was figured to be a major cog in the Panthers' passing attack.

1 9 9 6

Receiver Mark Carrier caught 58 passes for a team-high 808 yards.

Carolina next looked for the player who would lead that passing attack and run the team's offense. Capers and Polian felt the team needed both an experienced signal-caller—someone who had been through the NFL's intense "backfield wars"—to get things started and a young quarterback to apprentice under the veteran and take over the team in the future. Polian immediately thought of Frank Reich, who had served as backup to Jim Kelly during Buffalo's Super Bowl years and had started in Super Bowl XXVII in 1992.

In Buffalo, Reich's specialty had been coming off the bench and leading the Bills in high-pressure situations. There were bound to be plenty of pressure situations in Carolina's opening season, since the offensive linemen protecting the quarterback would never have played together before. The 33-year-old Reich welcomed the challenge and immediately signed on with the Panthers.

Polian's scouts were unanimous in their pick for the best young quarterback in the upcoming college draft. They chose the big (6-foot-5 and 240 pounds) and talented Kerry Collins, who had led Penn State to an undefeated season,

Kerry Collins led the first-year Panthers offense (pages 18-19).

Safety Chad Cota set a new team record for tackles in a single season, making 153 stops.

the championship of the powerful Big Ten Conference, and a Rose Bowl victory in 1994. Collins had size, arm strength, leadership skills, and poise. The Panthers used the first draft pick in their history to grab him.

The two drafts yielded some key starters for Carolina, but there were still many holes to fill. Polian reviewed the players who were available as free agents, looking carefully for defensive leaders and special teams performers. "If you look at who the great teams and champions in this league have been, you can see that great defense and special teams will win a lot of football games," Polian explained.

To bolster his team's defensive unit, Polian signed on linebackers Lamar Lathon and Sam Mills, hard-rushing defensive end Mike Fox, and safety Brett Maxie. For special teams help, Polian brought in two top kickers: John Kasay, one of the most accurate field goal kickers in NFL history, and punter Tommy Barnhardt, who had played his college football at the nearby University of North Carolina. With a solid core of veterans in place, the Panthers were ready for their first NFL season.

A CLASSY DEBUT SEASON

Carolina became the most successful expansion franchise in NFL history. After starting 0–5, a win over the New York Jets in week six at Clemson Memorial Stadium triggered a rush of four straight Panthers victories. The most impressive win was a stunning 13–7 upset of the defending Super Bowl champion 49ers in San Francisco. During the streak, Kerry Collins became Carolina's starting quarterback and quickly proved he was no ordinary rookie. By the season's end, the Panthers had set a new NFL first-year record with seven victories, and Collins had made his own mark by completing 214 passes for 2,717 yards and 14 touchdowns.

Also starring in Carolina's first season were veteran wide receiver Mark Carrier and strong safety Brett Maxie. Carrier snagged 66 passes for 1,002 yards and three touchdowns and quickly became Collins's favorite target. "Mark is an old pro, and when things would break down, I always knew where to find him," explained the rookie quarterback. "He was my security blanket out there."

Maxie led a ball-hawking secondary that intercepted 21 passes. The hard-hitting safety picked off six passes and provided endless help to his younger teammates—help much

1 9 9 7

Speedy receiver Rae Carruth led all NFL rookies in receptions (44) and yards (545).

Shifty halfback Fred Lane.

Explosive linebacker Lamar Lathon.

appreciated by standout first-year cornerback Tyrone Poole. "Being a rookie, it's nice to know Brett's back there to cover my mistakes," he said. "He's taught me a lot."

The Panthers quickly sent a signal to the rest of the league that, as British general Cornwallis had discovered more than 200 years earlier, teams were going to run into a hornet's nest when they came to Carolina to do battle.

THE PANTHERS' NEW LAIR

1 9 9 7

Cornerback Eric Davis made five interceptions and broke up a team-high 23 passes.

Every NFL team counts heavily on having a home-field advantage. Friendly surroundings, vocal fans, and familiar bounces all give home teams an edge. For the first-year Panthers, Clemson University's Memorial Stadium provided a suitable place to get their feet wet, but it wasn't quite home. "We got off to a real good start in Clemson," said linebacker Lamar Lathon, "but I think most of the guys can't wait to get into the new stadium."

In 1996, the Panthers moved into their real home: sparkling new Ericsson Stadium. Built on 33 acres in uptown Charlotte, the 73,250-seat facility gleamed Carolina black, blue, and silver. "It's very special," said New England Patriots owner Robert Kraft. "This is the future and the prototype of what every NFL city should have." The $187-million facility offered Carolina fans many unique features. The stadium's front row of sideline seats are located a mere 50 feet from the action, and all seats are angled directly toward the center of the field to provide the best possible viewing.

Outside the stadium, the entrances are guarded by six massive bronze panthers, whose fierce expressions let visiting teams know they are in for a fight. "I love the big cats," tackle Blake Brockermeyer said of the eight-foot statues. "It makes the place look mean."

Opposing squads soon learned the hard way just how mean the Panthers were in their new home. Carolina went undefeated in eight regular-season home games at Ericsson Stadium on its way to a stunning 12–4 second-season record. Playing in front of sellout crowds, the Panthers usually blew out opponents by double-digit margins. "From the moment you walk into this place, you feel invincible," Panthers linebacker Kevin Greene said. "The fans just won't let us lose."

With the support of its intimidating home field advantage, the Panthers made the unlikely transition from struggling expansion team to NFL powerhouse.

1 9 9 8

All-Pro tight end Wesley Walls snagged 49 passes for 506 yards and five touchdowns.

THE "FIELD MOUSE" TAKES CHARGE

When general manager Bill Polian had built the first Panthers team, he selected the veterans he signed on very carefully. "We didn't want older guys in here who were just playing out the string," he explained. "We wanted guys who knew how to win, still wanted to win, and could teach the young guys what they had to do to get there." With those criteria in mind, Polian had signed four-time Pro-Bowl middle linebacker Sam Mills to a free-agent contract.

At first, many experts thought that the signing was a mistake. Although Mills had been one of the league's finest defenders for nearly a decade, he was already 36 years old—a dinosaur in the tough world of linebackers. Those experts should have known better than to bet against the fiercely proud Mills, who had spent his entire professional career proving people wrong.

Coming out of New Jersey's tiny Montclair State University in 1981, Mills was considered to be a long shot professional prospect at best. At 5-foot-9 and 230 pounds, many scouts thought he was too small to handle the rough-and-tumble duties of an NFL middle linebacker.

Tackle Sean Gilbert made 89 tackles and six sacks— both team records among linemen.

Mills failed to catch on with any NFL or Canadian Football League team after college and took a job teaching high school in New Jersey. In 1984, Mills was given another chance when a new professional league called the United States Football League began play. Given a tryout with the Philadelphia Stars, Mills impressed the team's defensive co-ordinator, Dom Capers, with his intelligence, ferocity, and consistency. "I kept telling myself not to like him, because he was too small," remembered Capers. "But after watching him knock the stuffing out of guys for two weeks, I knew I had to give him a shot."

When the USFL folded three seasons later, Capers—who had just landed a job with the New Orleans Saints—took the linebacker with him. The "Field Mouse," as his teammates nicknamed him, averaged more than 100 tackles a season during his time with the Saints and was clearly the team's defensive leader. But after nine stellar seasons, the Saints felt Mills was too old and let him sign on with Carolina. "I didn't know what Sam had left in the tank," remembered Carolina nose tackle Greg Kragen. "But two days into training camp, I knew he would be our leader."

Mills shocked the experts by leading the Panthers defense in 1995 with 130 tackles. His nose for the big play also led to

Kevin Greene, one of the NFL's all-time sacks leaders (pages 26-27).

five interceptions, one of which he ran back for a touchdown to seal the franchise's first victory, a 26–15 decision over the New York Jets.

In 1996, Mills led a smothering defense that included fleet cornerback Eric Davis and hard-hitting linebacker Kevin Greene. The stingy Panthers allowed only 56 total points over the last eight games of the season, finishing with an astounding 12–4 record and the NFC West title.

Mills and the Panthers stormed past the Dallas Cowboys 26–17 in the first round of the playoffs. Carolina's amazing run would end just short of the Super Bowl, however, as the Panthers fell 30–13 to the Green Bay Packers in the NFC championship game. "It hurts to lose," said Mills, "but I'm so proud of these guys."

1 9 9 8

Halfback Tim Biakabutuka was a central part of the offense, gaining 565 total yards.

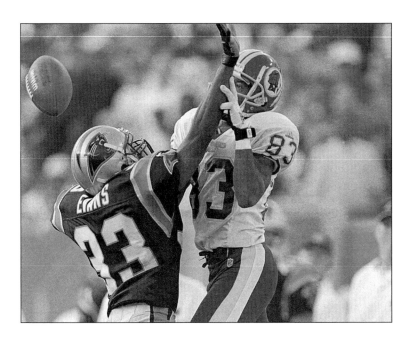

Outstanding cornerback Doug Evans.

Mills returned to play in 1997 at the age of 39 and again led the defense, notching 99 tackles. But the Panthers, plagued by injuries and a sputtering offense, slumped to 7–9. At the end of the season, the heart and soul of the Panthers retired. Mills went on to become the first player ever inducted into the Panthers Hall of Honor.

SEIFERT SHAPES THE FUTURE

In 1998, the Panthers' fortunes continued to slide. A host of crippling injuries and personnel turmoil led to a painful 4–12 campaign. At the end of the season, Dom Capers was fired as head coach and replaced by an old division foe, George Seifert.

Seifert had coached the San Francisco 49ers from 1989 to 1996, guiding his teams to two Super Bowl victories and a .755 winning percentage—the best coaching mark in NFL history. After leaving San Francisco, Seifert worked in television broadcasting for a couple of years before the coaching itch brought him back to the NFL sidelines. "I'm so excited to be coaching again," said the Panthers' new head man. "This organization is committed to winning, and it's my job to make sure that happens."

Seifert's rebuilding effort revolved around invigorating an offense that had turned sluggish after 1996. Fortunately, Seifert had a number of offensive weapons and defensive anchors around which to build. Young running backs Fred Lane and Tim Biakabutuka formed a solid backfield. At tight end, the Panthers had one of football's best in sure-handed Wesley Walls, and receiver Muhsin Muhammad had shown signs of

1 9 9 9

Quarterback Steve Beuerlein was named to his first Pro Bowl after passing for 4,436 yards.

Big-play receiver Muhsin Muhammad.

Carolina's all-time interceptions leader, Eric Davis.   31

The Panthers relied on receiver Patrick Jeffers as a key offensive weapon.

brilliance. The team also had a strong defensive lineup led by cornerback Doug Evans and massive tackle Sean Gilbert.

Although Carolina started the 1999 season 2–5, Seifert's leadership soon began to pay off. The Panthers won six of their last nine games, narrowly missing the playoffs. "It was a great run for us," said Steve Beuerlein. "A lot of people wrote us off early in the season, but our guys kept scrapping." The veteran quarterback was one of the driving forces behind the streak. After a struggling Kerry Collins was released, Beuerlein seized the starting job and threw for 4,436 yards and 36 touchdowns. At the age of 34, the former Notre Dame star was named to his first Pro Bowl.

On the receiving end of many of Beuerlein's throws was the speedy Muhammad. The 6-foot-2 and 217-pound receiver snared an NFC-high 96 passes for 1,253 yards. "Muhammad is just so big and strong," noted San Francisco 49ers head coach Steve Mariucci. "Once he gets his hands on the ball, he's hard to pull down."

Muhammad is just one of the many reasons Carolina fans have for optimism. After the season, Carolina beefed up its defense with the addition of several free agents, including end Chuck Smith and linebacker Lee Woodall. The young Panthers are rebuilding, but with a championship-caliber coach at the helm and some of the league's best fans cheering them on, it might not be long before these Panthers claw all the way to the top.